Love, Sex, Lies
and REALITY

Love, Sex, Lies and REALITY

Sean, I pray this blesses you,
Kemi

Kemi Sogunle

Love, Sex, Lies and Reality
Copyright © 2014 by Kemi Sogunle

All rights reserved. No part of this publication may be reproduced, stored in a retrieval system or transmitted in any form or by means – for example, electronic, photocopy, and recording – without the prior written permission of the publisher. The only exception is brief quotations in printed reviews. If you will like to use material from the book (other than for review purposes), prior written permission must be obtained from the publisher. Thank you for your support of the author's rights.

First Printing: 2014

Print ISBN: 978-0-9909721-0-5
eBook ISBN: 978-0-9909721-1-2

Cover design by Jeanine Henning

Book design by Maureen Cutajar,
www.gopublished.com

This book is dedicated to my love, my life and my miracle, Tobi. Thank you for always motivating me and making me the best mom and friend. I love you always.

Acknowledgements

Life is a journey with many processes and rivers to cross. Without God, I am nothing and would notbe able to walk this journey. To the One who gave me life, His breathe and showers me with abundant love. He chose me before I was born and He grants me grace to live each day. To God be the Glory now and forever more.

I thank my late dad, Nathaniel Abiodun Sogunle, who indirectly taught me to write, may you continue to rest in the Lord. To my mom and siblings, I say thank you.

I have met and continue to meet so many beautiful souls as I walk through my journey – those who constantly motivate, encourage and support me in all I do. To my friends who pushed me constantly to write (you all know who you are) and all those who inspire me daily to be the best. I say a big thanks from the bottom of my heart. May God reward you all in all you do. To my guardian angel, sister and friend, Karen Marks, I will forever cherish our friendship and love. God bless you. To Mr. Ayo Olusanya of Kent Christian Radio Station, thank you for the help rendered at the very last minute. To Gbolahan, thank you for your support. God bless you.

Finally, to Jennifer Henning and Maureen Cutajar, thank you for designing the cover page and formatting the content respectively.

Contents

PREFACE 1
INTRODUCTION 3
NUGGET #1 5
Love and Hurt
NUGGET #2 17
Facing Reality After Been Hurt
NUGGET #3 25
Lies and Antics
NUGGET #4 31
Sex
NUGGET #5 39
Facing Reality
NUGGET #6 45
Tricks and Tips
NUGGET #7 51
Self Love and Development
NUGGET #8 59
About "Us" not "Me"
NUGGET #9 67
Bottom Line
ABOUT THE AUTHOR 73

Preface

Everyone eats an apple but oftentimes, we all have our preferences for eating it; some like it sliced, some diced, yet others baked while others may prefer it in a pie, make a cider or just eat it as it is. Love can also be viewed from different perspectives, yet real love continues to remain a constant. It never changes. We all just handle love in different ways while trying to figure it all out.

The same applies to sex. We don't all deal with it in the same manner, some like it wild, others like to take it nice and slow and better still, others love to explore different ways. We may lie to get it, deceive others to give it up just to satisfy our wants not necessarily needs and after all is said and done, reality kicks in. We all cannot eat an apple the same way but we all must come to realize it is just an apple and nothing more.

We lie to ourselves sometimes, only to get what we want in order to obtain satisfaction in that moment but it is not necessarily what we need. We face self-denial when we choose not to accept that a relationship has ended, yet we tend to hold on to a temporary situation…Love, Sex, Lies and Reality, it is all about the how we see, feel, treat and consume the apple!

Introduction

Experience they say is the best teacher. We sometimes go through life experience either by choosing to accept a situation or remain in denial of that situation. We want to love and be loved in return but it doesn't come easy. We lust, we chase, we yearn for, we desire to have, we feel, we admire, we salivate…we do all these things while trying to find "love". We may hide in denial, engage in sex, lie to get someone to love us but in reality we have to live up and live by the truth someday. Oftentimes, we get hurt in the process but may not necessarily know how to handle the situation or obtain healing once broken.

I have decided to write this book in nuggets so as to share life experiences based on observations, counseling others and daily living that may help you learn how to be the real you, preserve, accept, and discover yourself so as to prevent you from getting in and out of relationships too frequently. You may find me reiterating through some sentences to ensure you get a good grasp of reality and let it sink deep down with you….Love, Sex, Lies and Reality consist of nuggets that will help you understand what it takes to face and live in reality daily…there's so much to learn and learning daily results in growth.

Nugget #1

Love and Hurt

Relationships can be so simple yet complicated when the parties involved do not fully know or understand each other, coupled with their definition and boundaries of what they think love is. As individuals, we seek companionship right from teenage years and into adulthood. Men and women long for attention, to be in someone's arms when we feel down, lonely or when the weather gets cold (both men and women often get intimate to keep each other warm during this period). It could also be when we are facing tough times and we just need someone around us.

We often overlook some issues in relationships while focusing on the surface than addressing the vital things that constitute to the health of the relationship. We find ways to hold on to what gets us comfortable when looking for love and find out later on that what we think is love hurts (real love doesn't hurt – God never designed love to hurt anyone but to heal and help each other grow).

> *Women tend to seek for companionship and love in more ways than men. The key is not to look for love in the wrong places.*

When it comes to love, some fantasize, create scenarios and picture themselves with a certain partner – sometimes based on physique, good looks, status quo, etc. The focus on such however may lead them into the arms of the wrong partner albeit leaving them devastated at the end of the relationship. When you focus on certain characteristics, you end up shutting down seeing others outside these standards and miss out. Not all those who dream of having such partners get hurt but the key is to finding someone who really will care, love and stand by and with you all the time with respect/trust while bringing out the best in you and ensuring that you are with who God designed for you. We however need to be able to distinguish between reality and what we need from what will satisfy temporary wants or pleasure. Here some assumptions made about relationships:

What Some Women Often Get Wrong About Relationships – Some "no, no's"

Right from her teenage years, a woman yearns for a boy to sweep her off her feet, kiss and make her heart melt away, hold and love on her but sometimes she goes about it the wrong way. She may be a virgin to begin with and want to keep her virginity till she gets married but once she meets a boy who sweeps her off her feet and convinces (or lies to) her about having sex, she gives in willingly without hesitating or thinking about the consequences. She may also be influenced by friends who have already lost their virginity in the process and/or are trying to keep up with their peers. She may also want to explore the sexual side of life.

Decisions made as a teenager are either due to being naïve at that stage of life, peer pressure or mostly based on emotions but a teenager must learn to think outside the box and make appropriate decisions that may either lead to life changing experiences or may turn out to be one of the best choices they have ever made (note: this may apply to both sexes).

Let's get started with a few of the things some women (including young girls) always get wrong about relationship with the opposite sex:

1. At the initial stage of the dating game, the guy always wants to touch, feel and explore. It usually starts with a kiss, then he works his hands down to her breasts, sensitizes her and eventually expects her to give in due to the stimulation she is getting from his touch. If she turns him down, he may get angry and call her names but later on show some respect for her knowing she stood her grounds. On the other hand, if she gives in and allows him to go all the way, they both have sex (which may be initiated by either party). The guy feels he has accomplished his goal while the girl thinks sex is a way of getting him to love her more (in most cases it is lust not love) and now she has him all to herself or has his attention. You have actually just given him a preliminary certification for easy access to your assets. He may not think about it or the girl afterwards but the girl fantasizes constantly about it and assumes the relationship is now stronger and deeper than it was before.

    At this stage, she may become demanding, seeking more of his time and attention. This may result in the guy dumping her hence leaving her hurt and alone while he moves on. Note that not all guys make the move to go on this adventure. Some will not even talk about sex or make an attempt to grab the woman but act gentlemanly.

2. You start getting attached to him, then you make it an obsession. You call him constantly to know his whereabouts when you don't hear from him. You try to get closer to his siblings/family or friends just because you feel doing so may strengthen the relationship but you got it all wrong. You may end up humiliated at the end of the day. Stop trying to find out about his family, siblings or friends, focus on him, that's who you're dealing with and don't become too obsessed about him either, it is too early a stage for that.

3. You made the wrong decisions by thinking you can sleep with him even when you hear your inner voice telling you not to. You go ahead and hop into bed with him then get pregnant hoping you can tie him down with the pregnancy. You didn't think of all the diseases you may contract during the process either. You break the news to him and he tells you to get rid of the pregnancy which is completely against your beliefs. Now you're stuck, he may walk away, you may be left to be a parent all by yourself. If only you had made the right decisions in the first place, this would not have happened.

These are some of the lies women live by when it comes to love and sex. Some women often ignore the reality and assume things will fall into place when it comes to love and sex in a relationship. Most men don't want to be tied down with pregnancy or monitored every second or minute and sometimes all they want is sex. As a woman, you have to know how to protect your heart, respect yourself and keep your integrity by not giving in too quickly. Reality is that love is meant to occur naturally and can be achieved when you patiently wait for the right one.

> *We want to love and be loved in return but sometimes it takes waiting patiently to get there.*

Patience can be rewarding when we take the time to know and understand, first and foremost the man in the picture as a friend. You will be able to decipher if his motives are genuine or not. Not everyone you met becomes a prospective husband-to-be or partner but you have to learn to figure out what a man wants from you while still at the friendship level.

The very first relationship can be a deal breaker or a heartbreaker for any woman and this often sets the foundation for all other relationships in the future. As a teenager, you are young and naïve, inexperienced, undergo peer pressure; you may keep up with the Jones', can often make irrational decisions when first signs of sexual pleasure sinks in. You may also get extremely emotional at times and due to hormonal changes in your body, you become drawn towards the opposite sex. You may listen to your friends who have had sexual experiences and feel the need to try it out even though you sense that it is not the right time or right thing to do at that moment. Talking to your girlfriends however make it seem so exciting, leading you down the trial path.

Teenage boys on the other hand are enormously sexually active and become interested in touching, feeling and engaging in sex which is normal at that age. When a boy is attracted to a teenage girl, he makes his interests known to her and may get turned down by her even though sometimes he may realize she is playing hard to get or standing on her principles/set standards (keep in mind not all teenage boys and girls venture out for sex). Let's take a look at Sarah as an example.

Sarah was 12 years old when her brother's friend began to molest her. It felt weird for firsthand experience and she wanted him to stop but he wasn't willing to. Every time she got back from school, Ben was always at her house with her brothers. He would push her against the wall in her room, usually behind the door where no one else could see them, grabbing her and fondling with her assets then walking out of the room like nothing happened (while warning her not to say a word to anyone or else he would deny such happening). She tried stopping him several times but he overpowered her. This went on for 2 years before Sarah started sedating herself to sleep as she got tired of the sleepless nights and keeping the secret to herself.

She often wondered what would happen if she told her brother but then she thought he may never believe her story and decided to be quiet about her ordeal. After graduating high school, the thought of her experience prevented her from dating. She later gained admission into college and made a decision to venture into the dating world. She felt compelled to tell her boyfriend, Dave, what she had been through but was afraid of losing him. Dave was free-spirited, loved life, cared so much for her and was very social. He was very supportive of Sarah but couldn't understand why she was sometimes defensive and withdrew when he invited her to spend time alone with him.

One night, he asked if she would stay overnight at his place but she declined (they had never been intimate although he tried so many times but she resisted due to flashbacks). He asked her why but she lied that it was against her religious beliefs. Dave mentioned that he respected her opinion and was willing to be patient with her till she was ready. He tried several times and with no success, he decided to move on after trying hard to figure things out with her. She watched him party and mingle with other women but she wasn't ready to give in after the nasty childhood experience she had. Dave eventually started dating someone else after he stopped seeing Sarah. She was left heartbroken thinking if only she had given it up, they would still be together.

When I met Sarah, she cried and told me she wished she had done what Dave wanted. I looked at her, handed her some Kleenex tissues to wipe her tears and told her she made a wise decision. She didn't really understand what I meant till I explained it all – She needed to heal first and rediscover herself; she needed to think of the "what ifs" - what if she had, what if she got pregnant, what if he had been sleeping around, what if he had contracted Sexually Transmitted Diseases (STDs) without knowing, what if he had contracted HIV? Would she have known any of these before making an attempt to give herself up? Sarah told me she never thought about all that, she just thought she loved him enough to want to please him and make him stay.

For a second, she thought if she had given herself to him but wasn't thinking about the consequences or if the relationship didn't go further after having sex with Dave. The "what ifs" should always take precedence when making decisions about sex. Loving someone doesn't mean you should give up or give in to sex just to please them. This is one of the lies told in relationships. The reality is when it is all over, regrets begin to sink in. Questions such as "did I make the right decision" come into play. It may not be what you had in mind or expected. It was all guilty pleasures and it didn't leave you fulfilled. What next, when he dumps her and leaves her broken?

What Men Sometimes Fail to Understand

Relationships for some men often begin with lustful desires whether we admit it or not. A man sees a woman's body as beautiful before he sees her soul/character. When a woman loves a man, she does with her whole being and emotions play a significant role. A woman may get carried away by first impressions and words uttered. Words mean more to some women than to some men. She starts to believe every word you tell her from day one without disputing. A woman who often trusts too easily will easily get hurt. Not all women are gullible but the weak ones usually get easily misled by mere words. All a woman wants is to be loved, cuddled and cared for. She often wraps her head all around these when in a relationship.

> **There are men who do care deeply about the women in their lives. More can however be done to make the woman feel loved.**

Let her know how you feel, let her know you care, express appreciation for everything even the little things. You may think it doesn't matter but it does to her.

Not all men will show affection. It is just the way they are wired but it is sometimes necessary to do so, not only when you're doing the "chasing" but throughout the relationship/marriage. Don't take her for granted either. If you know you're no longer interested in the relationship, make it clear by explaining in a way she'll understand and accept, then move on. Don't keep her hanging and letting her think you're still in her life for a lifetime only to be let down after putting her eggs in one basket. Don't be harsh about the breakup either, try show some emotions or at least approach the breakup in such a way that will not take too much of a toll on her while helping her face reality.

The "I" and "Want" Syndrome

Relationships have become more of the "I" and "Want" syndrome rather than "We" and "Need". Everyone wants to have a laundry list and both individuals often fail to reach an agreement on decisions sometimes. Some women prefer to have things done their way while some men are not patient enough to listen to the woman speak her heart. Some approach discussions with unnecessary arguments that go on resolved at the end of the day.

Relationships should be about two people coming together with the determination of making everything work regardless of any situation they find themselves. They get to know, understand each other well enough and decide to become committed to each other in a loving and selfless manner for the rest of their lives. Focus should never be on an individual's "want list". Wants are often if not all the time, temporary solutions that meet the present needs but may not carry on for a long while. Both parties need to center their thoughts on "we" rather than "I".

If you know you want to be in a relationship, you need to figure out how to contribute positively to the other person's life, love unconditionally, be selfless, share each other's goals, work together and see each other through difficult times.

If you happen to discover (while in a relationship) that you don't share goals and dreams, it may be time to re-evaluate your relationship to see if you want to continue or opt out before it becomes a pile of rubble. You should not think of how your needs alone will be met but also about how you both can be there, fulfil each other's visions/dreams and meet your needs as a couple, while growing together.

No one should set unreasonable expectations or demands that may never be viable or visible. No woman should expect a man to do everything in totality (e.g. be responsible for all expenses). Women must be willing to contribute towards the growth of the relationship and support the men in their lives. Some men on the other hand need to stop taking advantage of a good woman who is willing to do much. As it is known, a man should be the head of the house but can men drive their cars to an unknown destination without the use of GPS? Learn to let the "egocentric you" die off if you are such a man. Be willing to listen and learn to work things out with your partner most (if not all) of the time.

Some women describe qualities they "want" in a partner - good looking, handsome, hardworking, God-fearing, makes this much money, has a posh car, etc. The question is do they themselves exhibit some of these qualities or attributes? Before venturing into looking for someone who is hardworking, you must be one yourself. Looks/outward beauty should not be priority on the list; character should be amongst other things to focus on. Ensure you know what you need, what is best for you, what you're willing to give rather than get, before setting standards that won't meet your needs at the end of the day. Knowing what you need/deserve will help you face reality, evaluate love, and address lies you may have told or are telling yourself in regards to Love, and Sex.

If you are willing and agree to be in a relationship with someone, you must be willing to sacrifice your time and self, considering the other partner in everything you do. Communicate, discuss amicably; disagree to agree with minimal outbursts, set time for date nights, trips and other activities that will help preserve and support the growth of your relationship.

Cohabitation vs. Marriage

Some people decide to cohabitate with the hope that it will end up in a marriage. This can be a deceptive way of trying to tie their partners down. Reality is when cohabitation does not work, you are left hurt, with regrets and in pain. It will take a while to heal and start over again.

Cohabitation works for some but not all, same as marriage. Not everyone is meant to be married. If you decide to get married, ensure you love yourself, accept yourself, understand yourself after discovering who you really are. Only when you have done this can you truly learn to know, understand, accept and love someone else. If you both then decide to get married, ensure you are both on the same page in terms of goals/vision/dreams, can tolerate each other, accept each other's flaws and truly love each other.

Coping with Divorce or Separation

Divorce and separation can be some of the most hurtful experiences one can face in life. You have enjoyed being in the company of your partner for a while and now your relationship has led to you both parting ways due to irreconcilable circumstances or abuse. You may find yourself crying most of the time or being alone in your home while trying to avoid running into people who knew you together or running in to your ex.

For those experiencing separation, it is not the time to go flaunting yourself in someone's arms but a time to reflect on whether you are willing to work on your relationship and get back together or whether you are ready to move on. However before you conclude that the relationship is over, ensure you weigh the positives versus the negatives. Make a list of what the positives in your relationship were as well as the negatives and see which one outweighs the other. If you decide to move on, take the lessons learned with you and avoid resentment or bitterness.

For those divorced, take time to document the lessons learned, avoid holding on to your hurt, take time to heal, don't be resentful or bitter about it. Healing may take a while but let time do its job. Don't go rushing into a new relationship rather take time to rediscover yourself, accept yourself, rebuild your self-esteem if lost in the process and love yourself. What works for everyone is often different. Find what works best for you and stick to it – it may be traveling, going for a walk, enrolling in a gym (if not already a member), moving away from your ex to start a new life, etc.

Nugget #2

Facing Reality After Been Hurt

The last relationship left you devastated. You had put so much energy into it and gave so much of everything but it just didn't work out or maybe it wasn't meant to be. The signs were there, your instinct could tell it all from the very beginning but your flesh was just longing for a sinking boat to nowhere. It all started with lust. Lola had just broken up with her ex-boyfriend when Paul came along. She met him at a friend's place during a meet and greet but she got locked up in his looks/physique. She started talking and ended up narrating her past relationship. It so happens that Paul knows her ex. She talked about it all night long and he told her not to worry, everything was going to be alright. Before she knew it, they both started kissing and it went down from there on…the whole nine yards to a touch down!

She was drawn to Paul for all the affection and attention she got while sharing her previous experience that had led to a heartbreak. She had just been dumped by another guy and here she was getting entangled with lust, thinking she found someone who loves her by consoling her. Weeks go by and she moved in with Paul. The intensity of their lust for each other escalated in no time. She began to see the other side of Paul after a few months of living together. Reality began to sink in…was this the same Paul she met some weeks/months ago? Questions ran through her veins. Why is he acting differently? Why does he utter such comments when she's asking questions or engages in a conversation? Whenever she asked why he acted differently, he would convince her that he was just overwhelmed with work and apologized for taking it out on her.

This went on for several years and she finally stopped being in denial as it began to take a worse turn. She decided it was time to end her relationship with Paul. She had given so much into it but now feels completely burnt with no energy to go on. It was all lust and it had worn out. Lola realized she was not and was never in love with Paul but infatuation and lust brought them together. It was all based on Sex and Lies and never Love….now she is left with facing Reality.

It has been two years since she called it quit and now trying to start dating again but she is skeptical and extremely careful with the guys she meets. She tries not to judge or evaluate them based on her past experience but when she notices someone exhibit some of the traits similar to that of Paul, Lola develops a phobia and go into hibernation mode. She is scared of making the same mistakes all over again, knowing she doesn't want to lust but gradually fall in love and love someone. Wow, the lies, the lust are now becoming real…she is beginning to take positive steps towards making better choices when it comes to dating.

Never go into a relationship based on lust only. It will leave you broken. Learn to wait for love!

Abusive Situations and Healing

Abuse can be mental, emotional or physical. Any form of abuse however should not be condoned. The abused or victim may not realize he/she is in an abusive situation at the beginning but when it eventually comes to light, fear of the unknown or sometimes denial may result in such a person staying with the abuser. Some people go through abuse and decide to stay, thinking they can change the situation. Some stay as a result of thinking about what the society will say or the shame of starting over or being ridiculed by others while others may claim to still love the abusive partner.

It is becoming a norm for some cultures to recommend staying and trying to resolve the differences between both partners but often times, when you are not the one involved, it is easy to give suggestions that may not be applicable. Abusers usually are those who have been hurt in the past and do not deal with the hurt but shut it off, become numb or in denial that it ever happened. The abuser usually is subtle when approaching the victim at the beginning of the relationship not exhibiting any sign that will make the victim become suspicious of the behavior.

Abusers sometimes think they have healed but not necessarily address all areas of past hurt/pain. Those who have experienced childhood abuse are the most difficult people to find healing as a result of not wanting to open up wounds from the past but when they experience flashbacks may take it out on the victim who knows nothing about it. Abuse isn't necessarily about bullying to be honest and the abuser does not necessarily pick victims. Some of them actually do have caring tendencies often shown when the victim mentions leaving.

The abuser can be controlling, manipulative, quiet, and sometimes will isolate the victim from contacting loved ones either family members or close friends. Some of them like to be alone, some are players and some are social to a certain extent (mostly to console themselves). An abuser will want you to keep everything quiet. The abuser may also woo the victim back by showering them with gifts. No one can change or help an abuser. An abuser has to stop being in denial and seek help willingly.

If you think you are in an abusive relationship, ensure you get out before it is too late. Get help to heal, forgive yourself and the abuser, spend time alone to reminisce and deduce the lessons learned as well as the signs to watch out for in the future. Life is short, don't let anyone rob you of your life before your time.

Healing may take a while but learn to take a day at a time. Rediscover, accept, love, forgive and be prepared to take baby steps as you start over.

Before You Start Something New

The last relationship didn't end well so what's next? Take time to evaluate your last relationship, figure out what went wrong and what worked. Create a journal entry or memory of the lessons you learned from your past relationship. Take time to heal from your broken heart (healing takes time and length of time varies with each individual). Take time to re-evaluate and rewrite (if necessary) your principles/standards. By healing, you take time to free yourself from hurts/pains you have experienced, learn to forgive the one who hurt you and forgive yourself also. Redefine and readdress your needs and how to meet these realistically.

Leave out fantasy and focus on developing yourself, not making yourself vulnerable or seem desperate when someone else comes by. Spend time with loved ones to heal faster, do things for yourself and with yourself so you know what it feels like to be alone. Learn to visit places you have never been before, do things you have always wanted to do and take time to love yourself more. This is the break you deserve and a process to understand as well as discover yourself.

Define your needs clearly, don't rush into another relationship and don't make yourself easily available or accessible if it makes you vulnerable. Ensure you guard yourself against repeating the same old mistakes. If it means meeting up in public places to you get comfortable with each other and define territories, then just do it. If you feel you're not ready for anything deep, make it known. Sometimes it is better to preserve yourself and save sex for last so you don't get it all mixed up or messed up.

Think about it this way, you go to the grocery store to shop for apples. You pick out the good ones, some appear crushed or rotten. You ignore some but you keep your eyes on those that are appealing and you think will taste good. No one wants to buy bad apples anyway, and one bad apple can spoil the whole bunch. Same applies to love, sex and the lies we tell ourselves. No one wants to be in a bad relationship but we often lie to ourselves sometimes thinking, even though we don't like this person initially, we can make it work or try to change them.

Don't start a relationship thinking you can change anyone. It doesn't work and it will never work. If your instincts are on the money from the very beginning, stick with them and don't venture into the relationship just because you don't want to be all alone. Sometimes it is better to be alone than to be in a messed up relationship.

Take time to love yourself first, discover yourself, and know your limits; know your strengths and weaknesses. Find strength in your weaknesses. Spend them in developing, accepting and appreciating yourself.

It takes becoming aware of who you are, loving yourself completing and knowing God created you the way you are, to accept yourself. This will help you create room in your heart to love someone else. You need someone who will compliment you, share you goals/visions and dreams, communicates effectively, does not talk down on you but is willing to accept you just as you are without seeing your flaws or focusing too much on your weak side (this applies to both men and women). Learn to be patient…it has its rewards.

To completely heal requires not holding grudges, no resentments or bitterness against the one who hurt you. Yes it may hurt but what did it teach you? We always have to remember it takes two to tango and be in a relationship. You must have consented to certain things that transpired during the relationship as no one can force you against your wishes. Now that it is over, don't go monitoring how he/she is doing or coping since your break up. This will only lead to negativity. Just move on and put the past behind you without regrets. It may not have worked out but it may not also be what you actually deserve or need. See the good in the bad situation and be thankful! It may hurt but facing reality will help you heal quicker than remaining in denial or lying to oneself.

Sometimes one may be in denial by holding on to the good memories, thinking those will help get the relationship back on track. Reality is, if it is not meant to be for more than the period it existed/survived for, you'll only be dreaming and slowing yourself down from moving on. Focus, regain your strength, stand up and be ready to move on, knowing someone who deserves you and that you truly deserve is still out there waiting to be discovered. Take your time, don't rush or make yourself vulnerable but proceed with caution, guarding your heart and going in with your head. It is not an easy process but determination to get better and the ability to focus on forgiveness without resentment/bitterness sure helps.

Don't Rush the Healing Process, Take Time to Heal Properly

You say you have moved on, healed from your past and forgiven whoever hurt you. Yet from time to time you still put up posts on social media that take you back in time, play back the hurt or pain and allow negativity to override positivity.

The one who hurt you didn't know better but your moving on requires that you to seek solitude and time to heal, forgive, redefine, realign and emerge stronger. Complete healing/restoration is not a quick process but gradual. If you still have to exhibit signs of anger, bitterness or resentment, you may want to re-evaluate any area you shut down consciously or unconsciously so you can be free all together. Though healing is not an easy process, once you attain it, the inner peace you receive is priceless!

Move forward in newness with hope, faith and love guiding your every step along your journey. Your very best lies ahead as you proceed with caution. Find strength within...you are stronger than you know!

Healing From the Past or Childhood Pain

We sometimes shut off past experiences or childhood hurt/pain that have continuously been carried around for so long by becoming numb to such. Sometimes people take out the pain they have accumulated over years on their partners who have no idea of what they had been through and may or may not be aware of this. Before going further with a new relationship or continuing with the current one, take time to address any carryover from the past or childhood (don't shut them off but take a dive into what happened, forgive those who caused you pain if any, think about the lessons learned not why they happened and heal gradually). This will free you from anger, bitterness and resentment. It also helps you feel at ease with your partner and creates a peaceful atmosphere for both parties.

If you happen to have suffered from any form of pain in the past and in a relationship, please ensure you discuss with your partner who may be able to help you heal. If you cannot heal on your own and need help, seek professional assistance to obtain all the help needed.

Never shut off pain till it eats you up completely. Ensure you find someone you can confide in and trust, share your burdens, cry if you need to by letting it all out. No one is conditioned for pain. We all need to address it and let it go knowing we cannot change the past but we can make a brighter future out of the lessons learned.

Nugget #3

Lies and Antics

Is My Partner A Player? How do I Figure This Out?

Men and women don't become players overnight. Some have been hurt from a past relationship, from childhood and may not know how to handle or overcome pain hence they develop bad habits which may include looking for temporary solutions to help them calm down and ease the pain in that very moment. These may include drinking, smoking, exercising excessively but the most common method of soothing pain for some is sex.

Each player adds flavor to how business is handled but if you look closely, there's a pattern mapped out. It always starts with the sweet words, ensuring you get saturated with phone calls, love talks that make you feel special like you have always wanted, but all they want is sex as a consolation to ease the pain they are going through. The player may decide to hang around and become a friend who benefits from sexual pleasures you share or give (you may also be benefiting if you are craving for such attention). This may even be defined ahead of time before the relationship gets too deep. The player may express the lack of interest in a committed to a relationship in some cases while in others, he/she expresses the will to settle down and tired of playing (but deep down knows it is all about the game while you may think otherwise). It often depends on who the partner is but the plan is always well laid out by the player whatever the case may be.

The player is always calculated but you may be able to figure it out if you learn to decipher and read between the lines in the words uttered. The words should help you learn to proceed with caution and not rush into believing everything you're told. Sometimes with the player, words said the previous day are hardly remembered. You may just want to re-iterate through the conversation you had the previous day for clarity purposes but you will discover the player may come up with a different story entirely.

Often times than not, the player always wants you to keep the relationship secret from your friends or family and may not want to be seen with you in public or may introduce you as "a friend".

It is sometimes good to keep your relationship private but if it has to be a secret, then something is obviously not right about it.

Don't give in too easily, don't let your emotions take the driver's seat, try figure out what the player's motives are first and learn to check him/her out with known/trusted friends. Most times when the player finds out they have been checked out, they get upset and want you to believe them and no one else (hence suggesting you discard information received from others about them). Better play safe than later be sorry you didn't. The more you can get to learn ahead in such relationships, the less you'll get hurt. The more you can decode, the easier for you to keep your focus on what you need rather than temporarily satisfying your wants.

It is also good to know that you can meet a player who lives in another country. When invited, do not make an attempt to go except your trip and hotel stay are paid for by your host. That doesn't mean you give up anything you will later regret as well. If a player decides to pay you a visit across the globe, ensure they have their hotel booked prior to arrival. Don't entertain anything that will leave you with bad memories in your home. Play along nicely till you can figure out who they are. Players are willing to do anything to get you in bed and check you off their "to do" list.

Putting up a Façade or Pretending to be Who You Aren't... Know Who You Are!

Putting up (or living) a façade is like living next to the stream and claiming to live near Malibu Beach, CA or Seychelles. The only one who gets hurt when the truth is finally out is the one living a lie. Be true to yourself...everyone you're trying to impress is on a different/unique journey and working out their process by grace...live yours and quit looking at someone else expecting to be them.

For example: You meet a wonderful person who you think is ideal for you. You both start dating and he/she paints a picture of who they are not. Ed says he is middle class, drives a Porsche, lives in a pent house and serves as a CEO of a reputable company. Trina on the other hand, works as an executive for a bank. She seems to believe everything Ed told her except she keeps wondering why Ed doesn't behave as classy and rich as he claims to be. She really likes him and has been dating him for a while. Ed invites her out to spend the night with him at a local hotel but turned down his invite. She keeps wondering why he hasn't really invited her to his place. He always showed up late for dates claiming he just left work...Hmm, something just didn't sound right to her.

Trina decides to dig up dirt and find Ed's real identity. In the process of running a background check, she discovers Ed lives in an apartment owned by his ex-wife. Ed also has a child from an extracurricular affair and is actually not a CEO. He is currently struggling to pay child support and keep up with life at the same time. He is dating a woman who currently lives with him and has no idea of his real identity. She had the instinct all along about Ed but didn't know to what extent he had lied to her.

The point is this – why would anyone put up a façade or fake it? Why the antics? You have got to live up to reality by not trying to please anyone but pleasing, loving, developing and discovering yourself first. It becomes extremely hurtful when your partner finds out the truth. You may end up hurting others and most of all yourself.

Take time to develop yourself, learn to be true and honest, be sincere and stop trying to mimic someone else or keep up with the Jones'. If anyone will appreciate and accept you, they will without any irrational expectation or demand.

Until you learn to stop putting up a façade, become true to yourself while humbling yourself, you'll only keep deceiving yourself and it is just a matter of time before reality sinks in. Life isn't about looking good on the outside but a reflection of who you are on the inside and how your daily growth radiates from inside out for others to see and learn from you. Life is for living but living it has got to be on truth and done right. Keep it real, do you always…To thine own self be true!

Time Wasters

A man may like you as a female but he doesn't define the type of relationship he wants. It may be he just left a relationship and just needs to buy time before going into another relationship. He calls you frequently, you attend events, go for dinner dates, visit each other often but there is no definition of what you have going. You as a woman may think he is so into you and assume you're dating each other.

If you ever meet someone who doesn't define the relationship he wants with you, I'd suggest you take time to ask, know where you stand and be on the same page. If he refuses to define the relationship after you both have been seeing each other for some time, please keep it moving. He is just using you obviously or playing around so stop living in denial.

On the other hand, if a man meets a woman he likes and expresses this to her, she may not necessarily like him or may just lead him on because she is enjoying his company and not wanting to be alone. May I suggest that the guy does not shower her with gifts, take her to lavish places until she is expressed and responded to his request on dating? She may just be willing to take you on a wild goose chase either due to a friction with her current boyfriend or just wanting to play around for a while.

Reality in both cases is that these parties are pure time wasters, don't hang around anyone for six months to a number of years without knowing where you stand. When they are ready to move on, you'll only be left alone and heartbroken. If your instincts kick in earlier and think there is nothing in it for you, don't keep dragging yourself along just keep it moving!

Married and Acting Single vs Single Chasing Married

There are some married men and women who act single. They go chasing after younger/single men and women who may or may not know they are married. These innocent people may start to think there is a future in there somewhere.

As someone single, if you know your partner or the person you're dating is married, please call it quit. How would you feel if your spouse was doing the same thing? Will you be pleased or would you accuse them of cheating? Don't get married if you're not ready to fulfill your vows or be committed to your partner. Think about the children that may be involved in such relationships (if any). How will they feel if they discovered you were cheating with someone else?

Think about all those who will get hurt by your actions and try to remain faithful to your partner. If you have issues, communicate and resolve them amicably. If you're single, try looking for a single partner to date rather than destroy someone's matrimonial home for material purposes or for company.

Staying in an Abusive Situation

Some people choose to remain in an abusive relationship or marriage based on lies told to self – self-denial. Some think it is better to be in a relationship or marriage than be without a partner. This often leaves them bound to the abuser. The abuser in turn leaves them battered, bitter and resentful. In some cases, the victims decide to stay with the abuser due to fear of what the society will say and think.

Reality and truth is this: Better to be alone than in an abusive relationship that may lead to suicide, messed up emotional state of mind but learn to remain sane while you still have the chance. Love does not and should never hurt. If you find yourself in a relationship where you have to question your worth, risk your life, count more negatives than positives then you may want to take an inventory and decide what works best for you.

Nugget #4

Sex

Sex, sex, sex…let's talk about it! Sexual intimacy is an area couples don't usually discuss but assume it will flow once the process kicks off. Some partners may fake climax in the process just to make it seem they are satisfied but are not hence leading to the partner venturing out when tired of faking an orgasm or enjoy sex. It is vital to discuss sex with your partner so you are both on the same page. Understanding one's partner can help make you feel comfortable with each other and explore each other's body better. Ensure you both have a good understanding of what you like and are willing to explore so as not to make your partner uncomfortable during the act. This helps you both enjoy the process and pleasure derived from each other during the "do".

Men and Women Think Differently and it is All Part of the Game You Need to Learn

Men always have it calculated when they meet a woman. The first thing that comes to mind when a man meets a woman is sex, believe it or not! His first glance at you tells him you're sexy, beautiful, delectable…he begins to undress you in his mind and then approaches you with sweet words that will eventually capture your attention and make you feel like you're in heaven. He has got you wrapped up with his words, looks and charisma. Now your emotions begin to run like a never ending stream.

Women on the other hand, are more emotional than men (yes, men do have emotions but rarely show they do). We tend to get carried away by the looks, height, and swag. Hmm, he is well dressed up, his eyes and that look he gives you sweeps you off your feet. You lose concentration and cannot think straight any longer. You get engaged in a conversation with him, get a drink and kick off the night. He breathes right into your neck whispering lustful words in your ears and that's all he needs to get you entangled. You don't remember the lessons you learned from the past at this moment, you don't even take time to figure him out, you have been all alone for a while and now this man just seems to be what you need at the moment.

Here's another scenario:
The music seems right (either at the party or the club or wherever you met), you get up and dance. It all seem to be happening fast and you feel lucky to have been there that night. You exchange phone numbers and talk for a while and there was a click. He offers to drop you off at your place, opens the car door and may even kiss you goodnight. Next day he calls you up for a chat, you liked his jokes and he cracks you up real good. You agree to go on another date. You see him again and everything got heated up quickly. You end up at his place, all cozy and uptight.

Wait a minute, have you tried to check him out with people who may seem to know him, how much do you really know about him? Is he telling you the truth or putting up a façade? Is he really who he says he is? These are some questions running through your mind after you have giving him all the "sugar" he wanted initially. You may have listened to the lies you wanted to tell yourself about the new man. You were getting tired of being alone and he came right along at the time you wanted someone to hold you, kiss you, caress you and lust after you but not necessarily love you. He doesn't call you three to four times a day any longer. It has gone down to once or twice a week and he has all the excuses in the world.

Reality is: all he wanted was sex. This may not be true for all cases as there are still quite a number of decent/genuine men out there but they'll never rush you since they are also trying to figure out if you're a good fit for them and maybe the "wife" material they've been looking for. You also need to figure him out and know if he actually is what you need going forward. Remember you have to use the lessons learned from the past to evaluate the present and determine if there is a future. I know you may say it is not necessary all the time but things may just work out if you're open and willing to take risks when finding love but shouldn't it be calculated risks? Do you want to keep making yourself vulnerable? You may also want to know that some men are wired to get up and go, if and when you give up your sugar too quickly. If they hang around, it may be because they have not found someone else and sex is good. Look closely at the man's actions and gulp down less of his words…words can be deceptive but actions will always indicate if he has good intentions. Same applies in the case of the woman.

Most people are afraid of being alone once a relationship ends. Some opt for a rebound relationship just to be with someone even though it may lead to nowhere. Other may choose to be in a "friends with benefits" (FWB) situation. Some people crave for attention constantly and are afraid of not being in a relationship or have the thought of not meeting someone else. The phobia of being alone may often lead to you settling for less than your set standards or expectations.

Settling for a rebound may allow you accept things you normally wouldn't tolerate in a regular relationship. Both parties may end up consoling each other sexually while remaining unfulfilled whether in a rebound or as FWBs. FWB may also get you in trouble if the other partner decides it's over and you've been exchanging private pictures over social media but the losing partner decides to revenge. This may end up leading to blackmail of some sort. Be careful what you put out there. Pictures sent cannot be recalled and you may end up tarnishing your true self in the process.

I often suggest that people take time to be alone when a relationship ends. This give you time to heal, think, evaluate, redefine your standards and find yourself once again. There is no need settling for what you don't need. It may just be a want which when it ends, leaves you in the same dilemma as you were before.

For every relationship that never worked, there's a lesson in it for you. You may feel jilted, used, mistreated but the most important thing coming out of such is what the relationship taught you and making those into lessons learned for future you.

Every relationship has a purpose whether it worked out or didn't. Some to teach, some to build, some to break and reshape you while others may be to help you become stronger and wiser.

Got Game?

You say you love him and always boast about your romantic escapades yet you starve him sexually with your regular excuse, "darling, it has been a long day, I'm really tired and have a headache" but put on that sexy lingerie only to torture him. They say the way to a man's heart is through his stomach but reality is this: the way to a man's heart is through sex. It calls the shots!

If you plan to deprive him, may I suggest you wear "the granny jammies" or better still the onesie with the padlock sign that echoes your message, "my shop is closed tonight"? I know you think I'm slamming the woman but I'm actually not leaving that man out either. He wants sex yet he is not ready for foreplay. Brother, do you think a woman always wants a quickie? Hell no! You just make her feel like your game expired long time ago. If boxers turns her on, don't go wearing grandpa briefs. If you need to explore each other to help you both get back what is missing (if anything is actually missing in your bedroom game), do so. You have got to learn to spice up your skills in the bedroom department and please learn not to fall asleep then snore right after the do. Try spending at least some minutes chatting with her before you doze off. Communication flows well after sex without much argument.

> *Don't go complaining to your friends about how terrible your partner is in bed. Get on with your game and play till the break of dawn. When you give a man all the attention in bed, trust me, you can get to fine tune him as long as you keep satisfying him in that department.*

Playing the Sex Game or Hanky Panky?

You think you have got him wrapped up. He is all yours now. You have been together or have been married to him for a while and you can easily manipulate him with sex. You put on your best lingerie, cook his best meal, turn the lights down low and play his favorite tune. He walks in the door and you think oh, I'll get him in the mood. Problem is you may be banking on getting nothing…absolutely nothing! He may not be in the mood, he may figure out you only need something if you have deprived him of sex for a while in the past or have a lot on his mind. Men on the other hand, cannot be predicted. They want sex when they have the urge and want it there and then…no excuses. Depriving a man of sex is like placing him on hunger strike for months. Most men are stimulated at the site of the sexy woman…dressed in skimpy clothing, sensual/lacy lingerie or you're bent over in a position that suddenly arouses the man.

If you have lost your groove in the bedroom, it is time to get it back and spice things up. Remember when you first met him, how sexy you used to want to look every time you had to see him. Get back to that if needed. Make him prowl over you. Play the chasing game in the bedroom. Act out like a child who longs to be pampered and get the game on till you get him to the touch down line!

Men also have to learn to turn a woman on. Don't just try doing the quickie game always. Learn to spend time on foreplay, fine tune her strings and play on her guitar. The women should also not just lay down flaccid and expect the man to do all the work. It takes two to tango, remember.

To those hurting or lonely, don't go hoping from one partner to the other, all in the name of playing. Men often do so when hurt and use sex as a consolation to cover up their pain. Stick to that partner who is ready and willing to go all the way with you. Quit playing and make them fully yours.

The Energizer Bunny!

The energizer bunny is one who may never be satisfied with sex once and always wants more. It may be during the time you're cooking or cleaning. You bend down and he is turned on just looking at your rear. She hears the car pull up in the garage and she is all jerked up and ready to wind you up. Sex is a huge part of any relationship but both parties have to be on the same page about when it is going to happen or know how to fine tune each other into having sex.

You have to learn about and understand your partner. Know when the time is conducive and when it is not. Sometimes you need to watch out for actions and moods to see if those will lead to initiating sex. Sometimes it will require you talking to your partner and playing it out together than making assumptions that your timing will always be right.

The Couch Potato

The couch potato often wants to have sex but is not willing to do any work. This person just lays there while the other partner does the work (and may even complain). In the case of a woman, she either claims she is tired or she doesn't have the energy at that moment. She may even fall asleep before it is over thus leaving the man in "no man's land" to figure out how to cross river Jordan all by himself. Same applies to some men and please note not all men/women go through this.

My Time is Right!

Some men and women actually would not make sexual moves till they want it. Their partners may be dying to have sex but will have to wait till they are ready. These set of people may suddenly pounce on their partners unexpectedly making the partner become irritated and turned off immediately. It is essential that this group seek help if needed or work on ensuring they don't deprive their partners sexually due to selfishness or underlying medical conditions not known to them. Ensure you both are in tune and in sync. Engage in foreplay and work your way to satisfying each other. Waiting for your timing or when you're ready is a sign of self-centeredness and does not show your partner you care in that area.

Sex is meant to be enjoyed by both parties in a relationship. If you find yourself rushing to get the job done as a man and your partner is far from reaching the "first and tenth", take time to slow down and bring your partner along to touchdown. Both parties should be willing to share how you like it and what you enjoy most. Get into each other's games always and be willing to try something new. Don't keep repeating the same routine, you'll both get worn out of each other and become bored by doing so. Don't make it just a bedroom affair either, try different locations within your home. Be creative. You may sometimes spend the night in a hotel nearby or take a trip/weekend getaway and enjoy the moment somewhere different outside your home.

As a couple, it is okay to stimulate your partner with frequent text messages which may set the pace for what will happen when you both get home from work or later that night. You can also create an atmosphere that will lead to the moment – sexy lingerie, candlelight dinners, music must be right but ensure you're both in the mood and it is not one sided. Learn to get cozy with each other while sitting and watching TV. Learn to put your mojo on always that will help sweep your partner off their feet and get into the groove with you! Remember always that sex can be part of what breaks or makes a relationship and never be ashamed to ask your partner for help to assist you flow.

Nugget #5

Facing Reality

It may be tough to admit to reality when one is busy living a lie but the moment you embrace it and seek the truth, the quicker you face it, the faster you get to heal and learn to keep it real always. Pain, fear, anger, bitterness or resentment can cause one to live a lie. Hiding behind ego is another factor for living in falsehood. It is very much okay to address issues of the past and face reality so as to live up to one's expectations.

Addressing the Fear of Being Alone

A relationship ending may seem to be the finale of togetherness and what it seems to be like being all alone over again. However, you need to realize being alone can sometimes have its advantages. Time spent alone allows you to think about what you really need and deserve for a lifetime. It also helps you heal from pain, reflect on the past, digest lessons learned and rejuvenate. Relationships can be draining and time alone allows you to take your stand about where you really need to be than what you want for the moment.

It can be scary when you are so used to having someone around you, holding you and always there for you when you go through but as the old saying goes, "twenty children cannot play for twenty years". You have to come to a place where you face your fears and become comfortable with yourself. I always suggest taking time to be alone, away from friends and family so you can purge your thoughts and process new ones clearly.

Don't allow loneliness push you to the point where you opt for a rebound relationship or one that leads to nowhere such as "Friends with Benefits" (FWB). These types of relationships rarely have emotional connections. Reality is that in both rebound and FWB, there will never be long term satisfaction and there will still be room for hurt/pain to grow deeper than before. Both parties may develop feelings for each other but may have to shut such off.

> *Being alone will give you time to heal, think, evaluate, redefine your standards and find yourself once again.*

It is best to take time to heal, assess your previous relationship, document lessons learned while not dwelling too much on the past. Yes, it may hurt but sometimes you need to realize, people come into our lives for a season. When their time is up they leave, teaching you a lesson or two which will also help you grow and redefine you. Don't spend time listening to sad love songs but take the time to enjoy you while you still can breathe and have the chance. Embrace yourself, regain your confidence if lost and begin over. Don't stop dating and don't do pity parties either. Live life to the fullest and spend time in places where you'll meet someone...network if possible.

Self-love

Breakups, heartaches or ending relationships can dampen one's spirit. It may make you withdraw from things you normally enjoy doing especially when you feel annihilated. You may sometimes you lose yourself while trying to make the relationship work or trying to please your partner. You may need to rediscover yourself all over again.

Spend time going to the spa to rejuvenate, get a complete makeover if need be, go to the movies, clean out your space, take a trip, go on a cruise, take up a new hobby, fulfill something on your bucket list. Pamper yourself, appreciate yourself, love yourself, redefine and readdress your set standards/principles. Read them back to yourself so you are constantly reminded of what you need not want. Why do I keep re-emphasizing on needs and wants? We often get them mixed together. Wants are temporary and fill an immediate void whereas needs are long-term and are often met when we wait patiently to receive what is required to meet each need.

Spending time to find oneself, focusing on oneself, loving oneself creates room for self-love which is the first level of self-acceptance. Once you are able to do this, and accept your flaws or past, it will become easy to love someone else that comes along the way.

We sometimes lie to ourselves thinking what we need is someone who will help us figure out who we are and complete us. Reality is God made you complete when He created you in His image and after His Likeness. You have to accept that you are complete and believe, trust and love yourself first. Only then can you truly search for or receive someone who will compliment you. Learn to be happy with yourself first before you can make add to someone's happiness…discover and develop yourself while waiting for someone else to come into your love life.

Nothing as Good as Self-Love as a Starting Point

You say you want to be loved but you don't love yourself enough. You say you want to love but you find it hard to look at yourself in the mirror and truly appreciate, embrace and accept the "you" God created. You keep thinking there's something wrong with the way you are. Until you stop, take a look at yourself and see the real beauty that lies within, you may keep seeking and never find, you may keep mixing up with the wrong crowd while looking for love in the wrong places. Love begins with you, it is deep inside of you. All you have to do is reach for it, soak yourself in it and feel it!

Once you get so comfortable and truly appreciate your true self, you will learn to love for who you are….only then can you open up to love. We all have flaws and it takes the one who is meant to be to accept you with your flaws so love yourself and your flaws first, open up to receiving love and let love find and accept the real you!

Often times you go through situations you cannot explain. When you do, never focus on the "why" but the "how" and "what". How does this change my life? What lesson is there for me to learn? Your thought process often shapes your character directly or indirectly and can affect how much you focus on the love you have for yourself.

Take time to soul search and look deep within on how much you truly love yourself. This will help shape you and who you are. The more you love yourself, the less you'll allow circumstances define you and your character. Self-love helps you see circumstances as part of your growth process shaping you to become a better and more lovable you than you can ever imagine! Take time to love on yourself. Discover and develop yourself while appreciating the unique "you" God created.

The Playing vs The Player?

People who often play cannot tell you why they turn out to be players. These group of people hide behind hurt/pain of the past rather than addressing it. They constantly seek for ways to console themselves by exploring and engaging mostly those vulnerable. Once they obtain enough satisfaction to fulfill their wants, they move on from one person to the next leaving the former heartbroken.

Admitting to playing may require someone who can get through to the individual through constant talks or getting engaged in playing along till the player discovers. The player may also be blinded by ego thus refusing to see or admit to playing. You may then ask, can a player change?

The answer is absolutely yes! A player can change but it takes someone who is willing to confront and help the player get over his/her hurt/pain carried along from the past. Issues leading to playing must be addressed and the player must also be committed to change. Without commitment to change, the one rendering help will just be wasting precious time.

Heading Into a Relationship

The moment you decide you want to start another relationship after healing from the pain or hurt of the past, you have to be willing to listen to yourself, the person you're with, watch closely the actions and don't get carried away by mere words. We all know the moment a man sets his eyes on a woman, he starts to envision the sexual encounter even if he knows it may take him a while to get there. The woman on the other hand, may lose herself in a moment by listening to words that may mean or many not mean anything to the man.

The key is to learn to decipher while your partner speaks. You may not pick a lot but you will definitely pick something up within the first few weeks of dating each other. Do not seek assurance at the very beginning. It may appear to be a sign of desperation or dependency on your partner. Become friends first, don't lose yourself in the process but stay focused and alert. Let things play out gradually and you'll be able to tell if the relationship will last or not. Learn to be the real you at all times. If it is what God meant for you, both of you will share each other's purpose, share chemistry (not physical), compliment each other and it would feel like you have known each other for so long.

Nugget #6

Tricks and Tips

For Women:

- Act like a woman, think like a man - Go into relationships with your head, not your heart.
- The fact that he puts your picture up on his profile on social media doesn't necessarily mean anything or mean he is ready to settle down with you, it may be a test for you or he is expecting his friends to evaluate you. Don't get too sentimental/emotional or hyped up if it is just dating stage.
- If you have your status set to "in a relationship" on social media, ensure you're not in one all by yourself...if he is tagged in your pics and he removes the tags, that a sign you're in one all by yourself!
- Don't be playing "wife" when you're not yet one. Save yourself the heartbreak. Don't be used...know your role.
- Don't question him about his female friends...you're not Mrs. If you are, remember he had female friends before you so know your place. If he is not married to you yet, he may be exploring all options so don't become a "monitoring spirit".

Don't give up what you'll later regret. Stick with your standards and don't settle for less. Better to be alone than to be in a mess. Don't act desperate either.

- If you know your sugar is all he wants, give him salt instead. Don't give him sugar and later cry about being hurt or heart-broken.
- Don't be fooled by his status quo either...study is character instead, neither by his words...watch his actions.
- Remember you're made beautiful and complete...all you need is a compliment.
- Develop you, love you, accept you and do you.
- Know when a guy is no longer into you. Don't waste your time hanging around thinking you can make things work or change. Learn to respect and appreciate yourself. Don't wait till he starts talking down on you before you keep it moving. If he is always asking you to do things without making an attempt to render help, he may just be using you.
- Don't sit around a man who constantly refers to you as "friend" even though you both have been dating for a while.
- He doesn't take your phone calls immediately, don't call him back to back or replies with a text message that he is busy right away. If he has to wait a day or two to get back to you, it may signify he is starting to call it quit with you.
- If he constantly complains about everything you do, it may be time to move on. You may do everything right but he is never satisfied. No amount of anything can make him give a compliment, then think twice.

For Men:

- Before you play around with a good woman or any woman at all, take time to picture and see her as if she is your daughter, sister, niece or better still your mother.
- If you're still playing when you're over 40, you may have issues that need to be resolved or dealt with. Let your ego slide down the drain. Recheck your life, re-evaluate and address whatever is pushing you towards such, redefine and realign your steps/life!

Learn not to chase everything in skirt...everything in skirt may not be a born as a woman.

- Stop denying her on social media by removing the tags from pictures of both of you or posting her pictures for a short period to get her attention, when you know you're just playing around.
- Figure out what you need and stop chasing wants...wants are temporary. Needs last longer if not for a lifetime.
- Breakups do happen but try prevent them from happening by keeping your focus on needs.
- When ego calls, learn to let wisdom and humility step in...Think through and act appropriately...go figure!
- Stop forming or faking it. Be yourself always. You don't need to show your cars or crib off to get a babe...just ensure you keep it real always...we know some women are weak to fall for that crap but it is shallow!
- Don't ask her on a date to a restaurant you cannot afford. Always cut your coat accordingly so you don't go home and starve yourself. Stay within your limits and budget.

- Stop sending inbox messages to women on Facebook or other social media and pretending to be something else in the public eye.
- If you happen not to know what you need, try to stay alone till you do.
- Don't Photoshop your pictures or use old ones...that's outright deception.
- Heal from your past relationship or pain prior to dating someone else. It will help you see the woman in a different light.

For Both Men and Women:

- Never turn your relationship into a DVR and allow it record yesterday's events but rather take each day at a time understanding each other in a selfless manner. Rather than focusing on pebbles, channel your energy towards watching each other's steps and building on each other. Don't tie knots with strings based on weaknesses but look for ways to untie existing knots and strengthen each other...build bridges along the way and tear down those fences that exist. Choose love always...love covers multitude of sins.
- Never base your relationship on finances. When money is gone, there will be nothing to hold on to. Never base your relationship on materialism...this only last for a short while. Never base your relationship on good looks...beauty fades with time. Never base your relationship on what's in it for you...but on what you both can compromise and make out of it. Never make your relationship all about you...it takes two to tango...both parties have to agree/disagree to be on the same page and make it work/worthwhile.
- Never compare your relationship to those of others....there's a reason why you are you and they are who they are...your life should be based on who you are and not on that of someone

Tricks and Tips

else. Never base your relationship on mere words but let it be coupled with actions...always remember talk is cheap. Never jump into a relationship due to external pressure...it may leave you broken and worn out...learn to wait for the right time and the right one. Don't rush into want doesn't belong to you...you'll only find yourself rushing out in pain/hurt. Never rush into a relationship based on infatuation, it is only temporary...learn to love yourself before you can love another. Never go into a relationship thinking you can change the other person, you may end up losing yourself in the process.

- Don't expect a man to do everything for you and as a man, never treat a woman as if she is a maid or she is doing you favors. Every woman should be able to fend for herself without depending on a man as long as she has skills and gifted talents to put to good use. Allowing a man do everything may make him lose respect for you, make him seek other avenues where he may end up finding someone who requires nothing of him but makes him feel constantly welcomed. A man on the other hand, should be willing to render assistance to his partner within the home. Doing things jointly often result in a stronger and longer relationship. Sit down and decide on who is doing what so that things are clearly defined.

- Don't value other people's opinions more than those of your partner. Don't give outsiders an opportunity to know your business. Realize what works for "A" doesn't necessarily work for "B". Everyone is wired differently. The key is to understand each other and build on your relationship together. Communicate as often as possible and don't hold anything back from each other without discussing it. The more you hold back, the longer it takes to resolve, the more you're putting your relationship in jeopardy.

- Be open to constructive/positive criticism from your partner. It sometimes help your relationship and also helps you realize the little things you do that may get on your partner's nerves once in a while. While you may not initially accept it, take time to think and process what was said to you. If you find any truth in it, you may want to realign yourself and accept it. Let the criticism serve as a point of growth. Appreciate your partner for pointing it out to you. You can never stop learning about yourself and growing. However, do not try to change your partner just to please yourself. Let your partner be who they are and you be you.

When love speaks it is about "us" or "we"…when ego speaks it is about "I" or "me"

Nugget #7

Self Love and Development

First things first…to be loved and to love!

You say you want to be loved but are not ready to go all the way to love or with love. You want someone who will listen but are you willing to listen? You want them to give their all but are you willing to give your all?

Love has to be unconditional, guiltless, selfless, remembering no past or wrongs. Love cannot be easily angered, it is compassionate; it tolerates and accepts.

You have to be willing to go through and to all extent without finding anything to complain about when you truly love someone.

You look beyond everything to enable you see the beauty that lies within the soul you love. Only then can you love and be loved in return.

It is often said you are what you attract but the truth is you are what you accept. When you accept to love someone, you accept to love them the way they are (their flaws inclusive). If you have to complain, then maybe you're in for the wrong reasons. Both parties have to be completely and fully devoted to loving unconditionally. If it is one sided, it would not work!

During the dating process, you have to ensure you pay very close attention and communicate whatever issues or what may bother you with your partner. If communicating your concern is missed at this stage, you end up being responsible for what you accept when you get engaged and eventually marry each other. Don't settle for what you cannot tolerate just because you don't want to be alone or seem desperate. Focus on needs than wants. The one you need may still be out there while you dealing with the one you want for the moment. Take your time to love yourself more. When you met someone, ensure you can love them for who they are not what they have or what you think you want them to be. You have to love to be able to receive love the way you envision it.

Reality is: When you are conditioned to love "unconditionally", be prepared to get hurt because not everyone is conditioned the way you are. Some will hurt you as part of the process to test you and help you grow. Sometimes hurt may be due to your lack of impatience in waiting for the one you truly deserve. Nevertheless, don't dwell on it or remain bitter about it…just take the lessons from it and be willing to accept what happened. Ensure you remain true to yourself, continue to develop yourself, trust yourself and be patient enough to wait for and receive the one who is designed to respond with the unconditional love.

If you keep focusing on what you want, you may miss out on what you need. When you love yourself completely and love shows up at your door step, you will be able to accept love based on your needs. Not everyone that comes by, will be the love you need but it is up to you to decipher and be cautious of what and who you let in. Ensure you let out all baggage you may also be carrying from the past as these may hinder you for realizing when love arrives.

Be Comfortable in Your Own Company

We often think it is only the women who need to take time to be alone but men also need to learn to be alone. Men are quick to hop into short term relationships till they finally find what suits them (not factoring if they hurt others in the process and this sometimes also apply to women). At the end of a relationship, learn to be comfortable in your own company without having anyone around you or discussing your issues with anyone. When you're comfortable in your own company and skin, you won't fall for anything that will serve as a temporary solution or source of comfort but will have the ability to focus on long term goals and needs.

We often seek or long for company which is the main reason why we settle for relationships that end up breaking us all together. The moment you become comfortable with yourself and learn to enjoy your own company, the more you begin to realize the need to become friends first when it comes to relationships with the opposite sex. Becoming friends will help you recognize if the relationship is worth taking a step forward to the next level, if it is what both of you need and if your long term goals and needs will be met. This may also help you discover more about yourself when it is still at the friendship level.

Set Standards

Everyone should have a set of standards in order to avoid falling for anyone who comes along. It is very much okay to also have some expectations but not aim too high. Start by listing your goals/dreams/visions, how you hope to meet those, define what you are looking for in a partner and write down how your definition ties back to your goals/dreams/visions. List attributes that make up the character of who you are looking to be with and spend the rest of your life with. Physical appearance should be put at the end of the list.

Beauty without character is vain as we all know. However, do not raise your standards beyond who you really are and what defines you. You should not want a man with a good job when you're nowhere close to that or don't have a job at all. I'm not saying you cannot dream big but it is appropriate to cut your coat according to your own size. Don't judge by appearance either. Appearance and looks can be quite deceiving but once you can fully know and understand someone's character, you should be able to conclude whether he/she is what you need and deserve.

Never fall for a person's image and status as they may serve as a false representation of character. Watch closely the character and you'll know who a person really is.

Learning to Trust Again

Trust is often complicated and can be based on past experiences, values and expectations. Trust can be based on life lessons that help and shape you as you start to develop and value yourself more. It can also depend on what you believe and accept as wrong or right. It also depends on your self-esteem and set expectations. You must be confident in and with yourself. Don't expect too much of anyone than you will of yourself.

You can rebuild and regain someone's trust by knowing that life sometimes requires you to take a risk but at the same time be willing to accept the outcome based on expectations you set when you decided to accept the risk. Don't let it lower your self-esteem either. Learn to be consistent and not settle for anything less than your set standards due to desperation or fear of being alone.

Fear can also prevent you from learning to trust again. Fear will remind you of the betrayal of trust every time you make an attempt to rebuild trust but when you allow love overshadow fear, you may actually help your partner overcome while rebuilding your relationship (if it is meant to be). If you decided to move on to another relationship, ensure you don't allow fear debar you from trusting your new partner and also make sure you don't carry the hurt due to breach of trust in your old relationship into the new one. Don't allow fear prevent you from learning to trust again and don't let your past dictate your present or future.

Food for thought

Not everyone who started your journey with you will finish with you. There are those who are meant for the beginning, passersby, those who will help you transition, those who will challenge you and those who are meant to finish the process with you. Be prayerful and learn to discern who belongs where so you don't place the wrong people in the right path and the right people in the wrong path (you alone will suffer the consequences for doing so - it is your race not theirs).

Don't Let Your Past Define Who You Are Going Forward

As you begin to develop yourself, learn to stop referring to or focusing on your past like you still live there. It was meant to lead and teach you going forward. Take the lessons learned from it and put them to good use. Feeding so much on where you used to be will only continue to take you back to where you are no longer supposed to be...if you were meant to be back there, you won't be where you are now...realize that chapter is closed and all part of the process. It prepared you for where you are now and the future!

You are meant to become stronger and wiser based on what you learned and going forward, you should never compare where you were with were you are now or where you're going.

Successful people never focus on the past but on the present and future (think about that). Be positive, focus and put your energy to reaching for greatness. Press on towards your goals/dreams/visions. Let nothing stop you and stay humble while at it. Believe in yourself, surround yourself with people that will motivate and push you forward. Your best years lie ahead of you! Let the process continue to refine and redefine you!!

Life cannot impose on you that which you aren't willing to accept. Don't let your emotions/feelings push you towards accepting less than what you truly deserve. Believe in yourself, be confident and stay focused. The best lies before and within you...it is all a matter of your choice. Choose wisely!

Learn Not to Be Bitter or Resentful

As you continue to develop yourself, learn not to be bitter or resentful going forward. The truth is bitterness grows gradually within an individual and often results in blindness/the ability to face reality while the affected party wallows in self-pity or become egocentric shutting down or blocking off the truth rather than addressing the issue at hand. You tend to hurt people more than love people consciously or unconsciously, when you hold on to resentment or become bitter.

The first step to freeing oneself from bitterness is to forgive yourself

Self Love and Development

for not knowing better and learning from what made you bitter. You may wonder what is there that you need to learn....everything that is to be learned. In every experience, there a lesson to make you grow and become better not bitter. Next step is to forgive those who hurt you or treated you unkindly. Follow this with love. Let love overshadow all the anger, disappointment and bitterness....starting with self-love. Learn to love yourself, appreciate yourself, accept yourself, tell yourself you didn't fail but you gained knowledge to become stronger and wiser. Believe in yourself as well.

Become better daily by showering and showing love, gain priceless peace within you, release yourself from pain and extend the grace you received to others. . Life is too short to be building fences, rather build bridges of peace. Life is a gift from God...live, love, laugh and learn.

Resentment just like bitterness, often starts off when you begin to feel someone who is genuinely sharing knowledge or exhibiting certain skills is better than you or you have been hurt by someone you love. Your ego kicks in and tells you it isn't right and you start to create a stereotype about that person which arouses the envious/angry part of your human nature. While you may think they shouldn't know better, you may miss out on what you're supposed to learn from them. They on the other hand, may not understand what your problem is.

Truth is resentment only shows a person is weak, exhibits complex and/or may lack self-esteem. Best thing is to learn to develop yourself, humble yourself and accept that not a single soul knows it all. We are all meant to learn from each other, not talk down, dislike or resent anyone.

Be open to receive and learn from others...in doing so you not only develop yourself but gain knowledge and grow in areas where you are weak. Learn from every encounter/experience in life even if it hurts. The one who gets hurt when you resent is YOU...life is all about learning and growing. Live a life of love always.

Make each moment count by choosing not to be bitter but become better with the way you treat and interact with others.

Love Is…

Love is an action…it isn't based on feelings even though expressed through feelings. When you truly love someone, you extend the love you have within towards the other person. If the other person does not know or isn't prepared to receive the love you have to offer, it results in hurt/disappointment. However, this shouldn't change the love within you or change you.

Hurt only creates an avenue for you to grow stronger and become wiser at giving love not to the wrong person especially when seeking a life partner. Take time to study, know and understand yourself, extend/apply the love within to yourself sincerely…only after healing and doing this should you be prepared to extend love to someone who will be willing to receive and reciprocate the love.

Nugget #8

About "Us" not "Me"

Finding a Partner who Understands and Shares Your Purpose

We are all created for a purpose and we embark on our journey in life working out our processes to fulfill our purpose. When in search of a partner, ensure it is a partner who believes and shares the same purpose with you. They encourage, motivate and help you attain your purpose to a higher level than you may have initially envisaged. They inspire and assist you in achieving your purpose without negativity but positively speaking life to your purpose on daily basis this you accomplish it.

Find someone who understands you and you can communicate with easily. Communication is very vital in any relationship, not just surface communication but in depth. You have to be able to discuss, dissect and digest anything with your partner. You have to make sure it is someone who listens, without judging or constantly talking down at you. Relationships alone can be complex but ensuring communication is smooth is essential to keeping the relationship going.

Ensure you are both compatible and share chemistry. Chemistry does not have to be physical or sexual. It usually has to do with both parties being in sync most if not all of the time. Compatibility is also essential. You may find a partner who has chemistry but you are not compatible. Find someone who is into what you are into so that you both blend and compliment each other fully. Often times you can tell if someone is not compatible with you at the very beginning. That irritating and annoying behavior exhibited is evident and always shows its face. Don't think it will work out by patching it and deciding to go along with the relationship. It is better to wait for the right person to come by than rush into what you know would not work in the first place.

Don't look for someone you can control, manipulate or suppress you or your thoughts. Relationships are not one sided.

It takes two people who are willing to commit to each other, be dedicated to each other, serve one another and love one another unconditionally to make a relationship work. Don't make it all about "me" either. It has to be all about "us" as both of you learn and get to understand each other on a daily basis.

Trust in a Relationship

Where there is no trust, there is no relationship. A relationship can never be built on lies, it just would not last. It is important that you and your partner develop a level of trust for each other and not hide anything from one another as long as it is related to your relationship.

It may seem difficult to trust at the beginning of the relationship but both partners must learn to build trust gradually as the relationship progresses. Learning to trust each other strengthens the relationship and leaves no room for doubts or suspicious behavior.

Honesty with each other on all grounds also creates an avenue for trust and growth for among both partners. It should not be about one person trusting but both learning to trust and depend on each other for strength when needed.

Taking Care of Your Thoughts and Emotions

You may listen to friends or other people going through stuff in their relationships and this may get you to start thinking if your partner is doing the same thing you hear from others.

When you don't completely understand who your partner is, you may begin to feed your thoughts with negativity. This will sometime lead you to become emotional while thinking, which in turn may gradually lead you to snooping around your partner, become suspicious of every movement, sometimes get you angry when you don't find anything and maybe even influence you to start a fight that is not needed.

Be careful what you feed your thoughts. Learn to understand who your partner is, ask questions if you need to know anything - there's nothing wrong with communicating and asking questions (it is asking in the right tone that will get you the right answers). Don't let your thoughts and emotions lead you to become paranoid. Don't make assumptions either as they may become self-fulfilling prophesy in your relationship leading to you heading in the wrong direction. Ensure communication between you and your partner is always an on-going process and learn to do it in an atmosphere where you both can hear each other, talk without an uproar and obtain answers.

Communicate Frequently

Communication plays a vital role in any relationship. It is essential you do not hold back your feelings or thoughts especially when in disagreement with your partner. Ensure you communicate constantly. If you both have a disagreement or misunderstanding, settle it immediately and don't let it carry over for long. In as much as communication is needed every day in your relationship, do not allow a third person to be the voice for you both. Do not discuss your relationship with an outsider – family or friends.

Learn to let your relationship be between the two of you. Don't make your business other people's talk about town. The less outsiders know about your relationship, the better you both can communicate with each other, resolve issues among each other and build on what you have going on.

Send each other text messages throughout the day, call when necessary, write love notes when you feel like it. You may think these little things don't count but they sometimes express the way you feel without you saying a word when face to face with your partner. Make use of your body language to attract your partner and to communicate sexually when needed.

When you communicate, don't make it about one person but both parties and ensure you don't exhibit selfish traits that may tear your relationship apart in no time.

Be Intimate with Each Other More Often

Sometimes a partner may become too engaged in church activities, work, home affairs or other things that they forget to take care of bedroom matters. Sometimes women use taking care of the home and children as excuses to avoid sex. It may even be that they claim to have a headache or too tired to do anything after all the daily chores. Men on the other hand, have certain moods/timing for sex. As a woman, if you know you have to do so many chores in a day, please try to get your partner involved and ask for his help. You may have been turned down once or twice but it is all about the tone you use in asking that will result in the help you get. Also, don't try to dress too old in the bedroom and turn your partner off. Ensure you put on something sexy at night to set the pace and mood. Don't wait till you want it or starve your partner. It is not about you but about both of you enjoying the moment.

About "Us" not "Me"

The men should not aim for quickies either. Learn to set the foreplay tone. Men are easily turned on at the sight of a sexy woman's assets but the woman may need to be stimulated through foreplay to get her in the mood. Both parties should be willing to ask for help when needed during sex – it may be to touch a specific area or to make a specific move. It will help you both on the long run. Don't just lay on the bed but participate and carry your partner along. Try talking to each other if it works for you during sex. When it is all said and done, do not just fall right into deep sleep but communicate, letting your partner know how much you enjoyed it and what you enjoyed most. Explore different positions and different rooms in the house. If you have children, make sure not to make noise to wake them up so as not to cause a distraction and kill the joy of the night.

Most men wake up with an erection in the morning while some women have the urge around the same time of the day and may want to get down with their partners. Don't deny your partner the pleasure of sex for selfish reasons. When you constantly deny a partner of sex, you eventually push them towards infidelity and will contribute to them cheating. Many may say a partner who wants to cheat will eventually do so but you can prevent your partner from doing so by willingly engaging in sex even when you don't think you're interested. Get your partner to help stimulate you into the game in such situations.

As a precaution, I will suggest that you don't use sex as an escape from loneliness or consolation just to be with someone. Having sex with someone not committed to you may seem okay with you but sex normally creates a deep bond with your partner whether you realize this or not. Casual sex may also not put you in a position to focus on what you need in a partner or allow you find the right person since it takes your focus of your goal of doing so.

Compliment Each Other Always

Words are powerful and the way you speak to your partner may make a huge difference in your relationship. Learn not to talk down on your partner but constantly encourage each other, speak life and use positive words always. There will be times when you get upset with one another but learn to keep your calm than express yourself with negative words that can hurt your partner or leave damaging effects on your relationship.

Speak the truth to each other at all times.

Learn to speak in a tone that will not lead to a quarrel or exchange of words. Always be willing to pull each other up when down. Encourage and support each other on a regular basis. Be careful in selecting your words so no one feels offended but with no lies either.

Be Affectionate

Affection seals the love bond. It acts as the cement that binds your love for each other and prevents you both drifting apart. Some men do not like showing affection – they claim it is for the weak at heart but showing your partner affection opens you up to knowing what her needs her and how you can best meet those needs. Same applies to women who do not show affection towards their partners. Showing affection does not mean you have to be sexually connected but it helps build the sexual connection while not directly tied to it. Affection helps you express your feelings, show you care and makes you both closer than you can imagine.

Learn to be affectionate with each other often. Cuddle up while watching television, share hugs and kisses often. Bring out your romantic side and help your partner discover missing pieces to your puzzle. It does not mean you have to have sex but it allows you both bond with each other. Throw a surprise here and there. These are all ways of building the love for each other through affection.

Date Nights and Vacation

As a couple, set aside some days during the week where you have date nights. This may be in your home, at a restaurant, a concert or at the movies. It may also be going out to watch a game together. Date nights create an avenue for you to connect if you find yourself drifting apart or feel the flame quenching.

You have to constantly look for ways to spice up your relationship and this is one of it. Date nights may also set the tone and pace for sex during date nights. When going on date nights, ensure you wear something appropriate for the night. Remember how you both got all geared up during your first date.

Women please get out the sexiest dress in your closet and set the mode for your night while on your date night. You don't have to go anywhere expensive for a date night if you cannot afford to and don't let it be a place one of you likes to visit always. Pick a place where you both will a some good time or a place that will bring back memories of your early days together not a place that one person feels you both need to go or a place you know you cannot afford but your partner insist you still visit. Both of you should agree on where to go prior to leaving the house so there is no mini-war in the car and the date becomes ruined.

Love never dies but the affection/passion you have for each other may fade over time when you don't personally connect with each other.

Spending time with each other while getting away on a vacation also helps to strengthen a relationship. Planning vacation around each other can be great. You can both spend time away from daily stress, work, family and friends. Once in a while, try visit places you both have never been to before preferably some place you don't know anyone that could be a distraction.

It takes two...

Ensure you don't put focus on yourself but always consider your partner in everything you do. There's a reason why both of you came together and that should take precedence always. Don't make everything about you and try not to take things too personal but learn to resolve your differences immediately.

The more you see both of you working together to make things work, the more you will be willing to compromise or meet each other's needs. Love requires sacrifice, selflessness, dedication and commitment to make it work smoothly. There will be rough times but never let those overshadow what you both have going. In such times, learn to draw strength from each other while also supporting and encouraging each other.

Nugget #9

Bottom Line

We all seek love and to be loved in return but the decisions we make when going to a relationship should be based on proper evaluation, knowing and understanding our partners that will help mold and shape our relationships. We need to learn to take time to discover and decipher the other party in a relationship. We need to learn to break down any walls built from previous relationships to make future relationships work. We need to appreciate ourselves first then our partners and learn to build each other up positively. Giving part of your soul to your partner should be done carefully so you are not left torn apart if the relationship comes to an end.

Don't drag your partner along if you have no interest in taking the relationship to the next level when dating. Define what it is you expect from the relationship at the very beginning so both of you can be on the same page. Don't deceive, just for the sake of sex while exposing yourself to diseases that may be incurable (think about this for a while). No one carries it on their head that they are infected with incurable diseases so ensure you know what you need before you venture. You may say there is the use of a condom but you are not guaranteed there will not be rips to protect you from these diseases.

Sex, Love and Lust

Sex builds a strong bond whether you know or not. You not only connect physically but you connect with/to your partner spiritually when you engage in sex. You may sometimes find yourself thinking of an ex when alone or in the mood for sex. This happens because of the spiritual deeper connection established with coitus. This often results in soul ties. Sex is deeper but loving someone is deep but not as deep as sex, so you may want to save having sex with the one who you love and who deserves to have you. You may also want to think of all the silent diseases out there and ensure you protect yourself. Some are however acquired even with protection so you may want to ensure you are with the right person and not just give out the cookie to anyone you come across or date…just something to think about.

Be willing to speak the truth in love with your partner always. There are subtle ways to communicate and finding the best way of getting your message across without the use of hurtful words may save unnecessary uproars in your relationship. Do what works best for both of you without comparing your relationship with that of anyone else. Don't get third parties involved in your business, they will only break the bond you both are establishing or have established.

Love and lust are not the same thing. Let love find you, seek love and love on love. Don't sell yourself short, don't act desperate and become vulnerable while claiming to be a victim. No one can force on you what you are not willing to accept. Once you decide to accept, don't go blaming the other party. Be willing to take responsibility when hurt. Forgive yourself and forgive the one who hurt you. Find yourself and know exactly what you need. Focus on your strengths and know your weaknesses. Don't go fishing in the wrong pond. Wait for things to happen. There is nothing as good as the right time for everything to fall in place.

Sometimes, divorce may occur as a result of not patiently waiting to understand one's partner but thinking you know who you are marrying only to eventually find out you rushed into something you didn't plan for or not what you needed. It may also be due to lusting after each other than loving each other. When the lust dies off, the matrimonial home becomes more like an isolation ward than a love zone. Both parties begin to resent each other or find faults that may not have existed in the beginning. It is always better to patiently wait for and on love than let lust rule. When lust dies, there's literally nothing left to hold on to.

Friendship Comes First

The best relationship between a man and woman evolves from friendship-building trust and understanding which eventually grows into loving each other while accepting each other's flaws (helping each other outgrow that which can be outgrown) and tolerating each other all the way.

The friendship stage helps you determine if you need to take a step forward (further growing into each other) or backwards (keeping it moving). Never make assumptions or jump to conclusions while still friends. Don't hold on to what is not if you see it won't work out and fall apart later on. Ensure the relationship is what you both need and you both share goals/visions that help develop you. Save the lies you tell yourself and deal with the reality so love can be built on honesty and sincerity. Never try to anticipate in any way possible.

Anticipating can be a relationship killer. It doesn't only raise your blood pressure but sets unrealistic expectations, causes you to over-analyze, develop imaginary/unhealthy thoughts, make you appear desperate (even when you aren't and this may lead to you sending a wrong message out) and may lower your self-confidence. Instead of anticipating, learn to reciprocate a phone call with a phone call, text messages, email or whatever method of communication works. Take deep breaths and don't rush to respond to calls, text messages, email, etc. Learn to understand your partner's view on anything discussed. Don't read meaning into everything or anything. Learn to redirect your focus towards other productive areas or find things to occupy your time...take a day at a time and let love flow naturally....don't force it.

Make Little Things Count

The very little things that we overlook or undervalue may cost us a good relationship. Little things may result in issues or may count depending on whether we remember to do or say those things or hold on to the minute misuse of words, lack of affection or disagreement. Whatever we do, let's do those little things that add to the growth of our relationships and leave out those that break them down. Take a moment and appreciate the little things that matter most.

Something to think about: Relationships be it dating or marriage can be viewed as "the needle and thread". You cannot sew a fabric with just the needle or the thread. You'll need both to get started. It takes patience to thread the needle and the more you learn the technique, the better you get at it in the future.

Same rule applies in a relationship. The more you study your partner and understand them, the stronger your relationship becomes as you'll have no need to fuss that much. You may still have an argument or misunderstanding here and there but it won't be as intense if you don't understand who your partner is. Learn to discover ways in which both of you knead and knit together leaving out third parties while building into one another.

Remember always, the needle serves no function in sewing without the thread. Build long lasting relationship not one that would break the needle before you're done sewing the pieces together. The real foundation of love starts with God and you should always put God first in your relationship. Let commitment, loyalty, compromise, faithfulness, respect, honesty and compassion be the cement of your relationship.

In All...

- Ensure you know, accept and love yourself sincerely before venturing into loving someone else.
- Communicate effectively and carefully. Discuss finances, children, bill payments and other related issues.

- Respect each other fully. Never talk down but rather lift each other up constantly, supporting each other in every possible manner.
- Be friends first, then best friends and finally lovers. Be sensitive to each other's needs, trust each other completely and be yourself.
- Be affectionate. Affection seals the love between couples. It helps bind the love and strengthens the relationship. Men oftentimes do not like to show affection. However doing so, makes you know how and when to meet your partner's needs. The more you appreciate and show affection towards each other the less you drift apart.
- Remember the small things matter most. Complement each other often, exchange gifts, dine out or go on date nights frequently.
- Have sex often. Reconnect frequently and never keep count of how many times a day or week you have sex. Keeping count shows you're both not intimate with each other.

How do you eat your apple? Sliced, diced or baked? Do you bite it, make a pie out of it or juice with it? Love is like an apple, we cannot all eat it the same way but have a preference for how we gulp it down applying different techniques to make sure we don't choke on it. Stick to whatever technique works for you, discover yourself more often and find ways to spice up your relationship. If you're getting bored, look for ways to bring in excitement, take vacations, organize and have date nights, explore all your options together and keep the fire burning always.

The greatest gift God gave to man is the gift of love. Love yourself first before looking for someone to love you. When you truly love yourself, accept yourself, know and understand yourself, it will be easier to love someone and be loved in return. Never give up on love and never stop hoping for love. Love is surely a beautiful thing!

About the Author

Kemi Sogunle enjoys taking care of her son, writing, traveling, counseling on relationships, gardening and doing interior decorating work. She also motivates and inspires others to be the best version of the person God created them to be on a daily basis. She holds a first degree in Microbiology and a Master's degree in Information Technology. She currently works as an IT Business Analyst.

Made in the USA
Middletown, DE
25 March 2015